DATE DUE	

Be a Zillionaire

The Young Zillionaire's Guide to The Stock Market

Charles J. Caes

rosen central

To Karen
Always there to guide and support.

Published in 2000 by The Rosen Publishing Group, Inc.
29 East 21st Street, New York, NY 10010

Copyright © 2000 by The Rosen Publishing Group, Inc.

First Edition

Library of Congress Cataloging-in-Publication Data

Caes, Charles J.
    The young zillionaire's guide to the stock market / by Charles J. Caes.
      p. cm. — (Be a zillionaire)
   Includes bibliographical references and index.
   ISBN 0-8239-3265-6
    1. Stocks—Juvenile literature. 2. Investments—Juvenile literature. [1. Stocks. 2. Investments.] I. Title. II. Series.
   HG4661 .C315 2000
   332.6—dc21   00-008946

Manufactured in the United States of America

TABLE OF CONTENTS

The Stock Market

You probably like to go with your mom and dad to shopping malls. And why not? They are convenient marketplaces where many different types of stores can be found in the same location. Clothing stores! Candy stores! Bakeries! Toy stores! Even places to eat, like McDonald's!

When people want to invest in a corporation, they go to another kind of marketplace. It is called the stock market. A stock market is just like a great mall, only instead of many stores, it has lists of companies in which people, including you, can invest. McDonald's! Hershey! Kmart! IBM! And thousands of other companies around the world!

What does it mean to "invest in a company"?

It means purchasing shares of stock in that corporation. Investors do so in hope of selling that stock later for more than they paid for it. If they can sell their ownership in a corporation like McDonald's for $10,000 when they paid only $5,000 for that ownership, they will make a profit of $5,000 ($10,000 - $5,000 = $5,000). This is one form of what is called speculation in the stock market. Basically, speculation means to invest in a stock in the hope that you will profit from a change in its selling price.

That is not unlike what the owners of those stores in the mall do. They buy clothing or other goods from the people who make them and then try and sell them to you for more money than they paid for them.

Instead of clothing or toys or cars or other goods, stock investors buy "into" corporations such as McDonald's or Ford Motor Company. That means they buy a part of the corporation. They become one of the owners of the corporation. Other examples of stock that investors may own are listed in Table 1-1.

Their ownership in any of these corporations will be represented by shares of stock. If a corporation issues one million shares of stock and an investor owns ten thousand shares, then he or she owns one percent of the company (10,000/ 1,000,000=.01).

Table 1-1
Popular Stocks

Stock	Symbol	Major Business
AT and T	T	telecommunications and business services
Bell Atlantic	BEL	telephone services
Cisco Systems	CSCO	computer networking products
Compaq	CPQ	computer manufacturing
Disney	DIS	films, television, amusement parks
ExxonMobil	XOM	oil company
General Electric	G	broadcasting, consumer products
Intel	INTC	semiconductors and electronic memories
IBM	IBM	manufacturing business machines
Lucent	LU	telecommunications and computers

At this writing, more people are invested in these stocks than any other. Stocks with one to three symbols are New York Stock Exchange listings, those with four are NASDAQ listings.

Many Stock Markets

When people refer to the "stock market," they are actually referring to many organizations around the world that provide the means to buy and sell stock in public corporations. A public corporation is one that is not privately owned and in which the general public, including you and me, have the right and opportunity to invest.

More likely than not, when you buy stock it will be through a broker, who, in turn, trades for you on stock exchanges or in the over-the-counter (OTC) market. So when you purchase stock, you rarely buy it directly from the company that issued it. You usually buy it from other investors like yourself.

You see, when a corporation like IBM or McDonald's issues new securities, it sells them directly to investment bankers. These investment bankers are usually giant brokerage firms, such as Merrill Lynch, Goldman Sachs, or Salomon Brothers.

A broker or brokerage is an intermediary—someone in between—the seller and the purchaser of a security. In this case, what are being sold are shares of stock. The brokers help create the secondary markets through which you and I can trade stocks. The term "secondary market" means that the stocks are no longer purchased from the corporation that issued them. Now they are purchased from exchanges or businesses providing electronically linked facilities all around the world.

Most buying and selling of stock takes place in the secondary markets. But there are plans by which you can buy stock directly from a company. In fact, your parents may work for a company that has a stock-purchase plan that allows them to have money taken from their paycheck every week in order to buy the company's stock.

Stock Exchanges

Stock exchanges are auction markets because the prices of the corporate stocks they list are determined solely by supply and demand. This means that if there are not enough shares of stock in a particular company for all the people that want to buy some, the price of the stock will most likely go up. If there are too many shares of stock and not enough people to buy them all, then the price of the stock will probably go down. The price of the stock is not fixed. Investors can offer to buy or sell them at any price they like. The buy offer is called the bid price, and the sell offer is called the asking price. In essence, the stock is being auctioned off.

There are many, many stock exchanges around the world—more than 150. They are in big countries and small countries.

Large and wealthy countries, such as the United States, have many exchanges. Among those in the United States are the New York Stock Exchange, the Boston Stock Exchange, and the American Stock Exchange. Just these three exchanges account for more than two billion shares of stock being traded almost every day. In the United States, the term "Wall Street" is often used in a general way to refer to the stock market. That is because the Federal Reserve bank, the American Stock Exchange, the New York Stock Exchange, the New York mercantile and commodity exchanges, and many brokerage firms are located on Wall Street in lower Manhattan in New York City.

Each exchange has different sets of requirements for companies that want to have their stocks listed for sale to the public. These requirements include, among other things:

 A certain level of earnings

 A certain amount of stock available for the public to buy

 A certain number of stockholders

A certain amount of financial stability

A certain amount of growth potential

Some of the foreign exchanges that you may have heard about are the London Stock Exchange, the Paris Bourse, and the Montreal Stock Exchange. Not all foreign countries have stock exchanges, but most do, including Argentina, Australia, Hong Kong, Japan, India, Italy, the Netherlands, New Zealand, Norway, Spain, and Venezuela—to name just a few. You will find a worldwide list of some exchanges in the United States and selected countries in Table 1-2.

Table 1-2
Some Stock Markets Worldwide

Exchange or Market	City	Country
Bangalore Stock Exchange	Bangalore	India
Belgrade Stock Exchange	Belgrade	Fed. Rep. of Yugoslavia
Bermuda Stock Exchange	Hamilton	Bermuda
Bogota Bolsa SA	Bogota	Colombia
Boston Stock Exchange	Boston	United States
Budapest Stock Exchange	Budapest	Hungary
Casablanca Bourse	Casablanca	Morocco
Chicago Stock Exchange	Chicago	United States
Cyprus Stock Exchange	Nicosia	Cyprus
Delhi Stock Exchange	New Delhi	India
Dhaka Stock Exchange	Dhaka	Bangladesh
Kuwait Stock Exchange	Safat	Kuwait
Montreal Bourse	Montreal	Canada
Moscow Stock Exchange	Moscow	Russia
Mumbai Stock Exchange	Mumbai	India
NASDAQ AMEX Market	New York	United States
New York Stock Exchange	New York	United States
Nigerian Stock Exchange	Lagos	Nigeria
Pacific Stock Exchange	San Francisco	United States
Siberian Stock Exchange	Novosibirsk	Russian Federation
Toronto Stock Exchange	Toronto	Canada
Winnipeg Stock Exchange	Winnipeg	Canada

This is just a small listing of the more than 150 stock exchanges around the world.

The OTC (Over-the-Counter) Market

There is also an over-the-counter (OTC) market, which is for securities (stocks) that are not listed on any of the formal exchanges. Unlike the exchanges, the OTC is not an auction market because prices of the stocks are negotiated rather than determined by auction. In the United States, the OTC is managed by the National Association of Securities Dealers (NASD), which is based in Washington, D.C.

Besides dealing in the stocks of smaller companies not meeting exchange requirements, the NASD also provides a well-organized computer network center for the trading of stock in larger corporations that meet special NASD requirements. This network is called the NASDAQ (National Association of Securities Dealers Automated Quote System). Microsoft, Sun Microsystems, Dell, and Yahoo are among the better known stocks that trade on the NASDAQ.

Types of Stock

There are two types of stock in which you can invest: common stock and preferred stock. You will find a summary comparison of common and preferred stock in Table 2-1. Most companies, however, offer only common stock.

Why do companies offer stock in the first place?

It is a way of getting the money to run their companies. They can borrow money from a bank to support their operations, but then they have to pay interest on the money they borrow. If they issue common stock, they may pay dividends to owners of that stock—but only if they want to.

The same holds true for preferred stock, though companies almost always pay dividends to owners of preferred stock. The point is they do not have to pay dividends if business is bad—but they

Table 2-1
Comparing Preferred and Common Stock

Category	Common Stock	Preferred Stock
Profit Sharing	Always	Sometimes
Liquidity	Dependable	Dependable
Voting Rights	Usually	Rarely
Dividends	Sometimes*	Usually but not guaranteed
Protection from Bankruptcy	Not so good	Better than common stock

* Some companies find it best to reinvest their earnings rather than to distribute them as dividends. They feel that by doing this they may make the company stronger financially and thereby push up the price of the stock.

will always have to pay interest to a bank or other lender even when business is bad.

What are dividends? They are a portion of a company's earnings that is paid to shareholders. For instance, if you own 100 shares of stock in McDonald's, and McDonald's declares a dividend of $1 per share, then you will receive $100 (100 X $1). Some stock investors buy stock mainly for the dividends that they may receive. You will find more information about dividends in chapter 3.

Common Stock

When you buy stock in a corporation, you receive a certificate representing the amount of shares you have purchased. If you buy 100 shares of stock in AOL, for example, then you will receive a stock certificate representing a value of 100 shares.

You always have the option of instructing the brokerage firm from which you purchased the stock not to issue you a certificate but to keep an electronic record of your purchase.

Common stock is popular because it gives you the following privileges:

 1. Protection. If the corporation in which you have invested does poorly or goes out of business, the most money that you can lose is what you paid for the shares of stock you own, except in very unusual circumstances.

 2. Profit sharing. When the corporation earns money (earns a profit), some of that money will be paid directly to you.

 3. Liquidity. There is almost always a market for common stock, meaning there is usually someone ready to buy the stock you own if you decide to sell it, though you may not be able to get exactly the price you want for it.

 4. Voting rights. As a common stockholder, you have the right to help select the top managers and to vote on important company business.

Some of the important company issues that you will vote on are:

    a. Who will be the officers and directors of the corporation

    b. How much officers and directors will be paid

    c. Number of shares of stock to be held by company officers and directors

    d. Changes to the corporation's bylaws (laws under which the corporation must operate)

Preferred Stock

Preferred stock gives an investor the following advantages:

 1. Preference. As a preferred stockholder, you get paid dividends before common stockholders.

 2. Higher Dividend Rates. While you do not share in profits the way common stockholders do, you will generally receive higher dividends.

 3. Added Protection. If the corporation goes bankrupt (out of business), you will receive your share of what value remains before common stockholders receive their share.

Some corporations allow preferred stockholders to receive dividends whether or not the corporation has made any money. And if the corporation skips a dividend payment, it will be made up to you at a later date. This is called a cumulative feature.

Other corporations, however, allow preferred stockholders to receive cash dividends only if the corporation has made money.

Some preferred stocks are callable, which means that the corporation can buy them back on a certain date and at a certain price. This gives the corporation greater flexibility in managing its finances.

But you must realize that whether you are a common stockholder or a preferred stockholder, a corporation is never required by law to pay you dividends—unless it actually declares its intention to pay dividends.

Types of Dividends

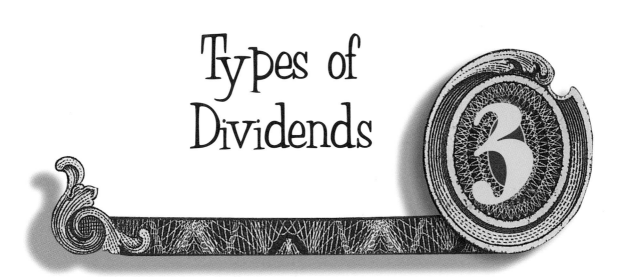

As mentioned earlier, dividends are payments that a corporation makes to its stockholders. Dividends make stock attractive to investors, and companies use dividends as one way to get you to buy their stock rather than someone else's. These dividends represent a sharing of the corporation's earnings with its shareholders.

But dividends may not always represent a sharing of corporate earnings. Sometimes a company will not earn profits but will pay dividends anyway. They do this in order to keep a record of continuous payments and keep the stock attractive to buyers. When dividends are not paid from profits, they are based on the growth of the investment that has been made in the company.

There are two types of dividends that are paid to shareholders: cash and stock distributions.

Cash Dividends

Cash dividends are payments in money to holders of a corporation's stock. Cash dividends are more popular with income-oriented investors.

If you own 100 shares of common stock and a corporation declares a $1 per share cash dividend, then you will receive $100. If you own 200 shares of stock and a corporation declares a $2 per share dividend, then you will receive $400. It is all a matter of simple arithmetic.

Dividend	x	# Shares	=	Money You Receive
$ .25	x	100	=	$ 25.00
.50	x	100	=	$ 50.00
1.00	x	100	=	$ 100.00
2.00	x	100	=	$ 200.00

Just remember that a corporation is not legally bound to pay a dividend to its shareholders unless it has actually declared that it will pay a dividend on a specific date. So if a company paid a $1.50 per share dividend last year, that does not mean it will pay one this year. But if a corporation declares to its stockholders that it will pay a dividend of $1.0͞ ͞ ͞ share on January 15 or any other date, then it is l͞ ͞ ͞ ͞ ͞und to do so.

Dividend͞s ͞ ͞ ͞ ͞declared any time a corporation wishes to share͞ ͞ ͞ ͞ings with its stockholders. It may pay them ͞ ͞ ͞ree months, every six months, once a year—a͞ ͞ ͞ ͞ ͞y times as it wishes, but it will rarely pay them more than four times a year except under special circumstances.

These special circumstances include when the corporation has had an exceptionally profitable period, when the corporation is trying to create special interest in its stock, and when the corporation is putting together a strategy to avoid takeover by another company.

Stock Dividends

Sometimes a corporation will pay its shareholders in stock rather than money when it declares a dividend.

If you own 300 shares of stock and a corporation declares a 50 percent stock dividend, then you will receive an additional 150 shares (.50 x 300).

If you own 300 shares of stock and a corporation declares a 20 percent stock dividend, then you will receive an additional 60 shares of stock (.20 x 300).

In the final analysis, only a simple knowledge of arithmetic is needed to understand stock dividends. But they are tricky, so read what follows carefully.

19

Table 3-1
How Dividends on Preferred Stocks Are Determined

Dividends on preferred stocks are determined by multiplying the dividend rate times the par value assigned to the stock. For a 7 percent preferred stock, 7 percent is the dividend rate. What that means in actual money depends upon the par value. Below are examples of varying par values and dividend rates. Note how the annual dividend is determined.

Dividend Rate	Par Value	Annual Dividend
7%	$100	$ 7.00
7%	$ 50	$ 3.50
8%	$100	$ 8.00
8%	$ 50	$ 4.00

More likely than not, the dividends will be distributed on a quarterly or semiannual basis. Thus, for example, the $8 dividend in the third example may be paid one-half ($4) in June and one-half ($4) in December.

The example below shows the effect of three different types of stock dividends. A 50 percent stock dividend may also be expressed as one new share for every two that you own; a 20 percent as one new share for every five that you own; and a 10 percent as one new share for every ten that you own.

Stock Ratio	Shares Owned Before Dividend	Shares Received	Shares Owned After Dividend
50% (.50)	x 300	=150	=450 (150+300)
20% (.20)	x 300	=60	=360 (60+300)
10% (.10)	x 300	=30	=330 (30+300)

However, though the number of shares you own has increased after each of the above stock payments, the total value of your shares will remain the same because a stock dividend is simply a bookkeeping game.

This means if you have 300 shares worth $3,000 and you receive a 50 percent stock dividend, you will now have 450 shares. But each share is now worth only $6.67 each instead of $10! The book value of each share is reduced, and there is a proportionate reduction in the current market value of the shares. The number of shares you own has increased while the total value of those shares

has remained the same, which means that the value of each individual share has decreased.

Even though you still have no more money than before, you have the potential benefits that owning more shares offers. If you received a cash dividend, you would have to pay taxes on that money. Because you received stock instead, you will not have to pay taxes until you sell that stock, and only if you sell the stock for a profit.

You will also receive more money from dividends that are paid on each share because you now own more shares. Also, because a stock dividend generally (but not definitely) increases the near-future market value of your stock, you will make more money when you sell that stock. As you now have 150 more shares than before, if the stock does indeed go up in price, you stand to make an additional $150 for every $1 increase in the price of the stock. (You will also lose an additional $150 for every $1 that the stock goes down.)

Stock Splits

There is another type of stock dividend called a split. Whereas a stock dividend affects the book value of the stock, the stock split impacts the par value. To understand a stock split, therefore, you must understand the concept of par value.

Par value is the value placed on a share of stock for bookkeeping purposes. It has no significance to the actual value of the stock, for the true value of any stock is what someone is willing to pay for it. For example, a stock may have a $1 per share par value, but its market value may be $100 per share, the market value being the stock's listed price on an exchange.

Sometimes common stock will be issued without any par value at all. In the case of preferred stock, however, par value has a very specific purpose, as explained in Table 3-1.

Now, in the case of a stock split, par value is also split, and so is the current market value of the stock. The arithmetic of the stock split explains it all. If you own 100

shares of Bell Telephone and those shares are worth $50 each, then you have $5,000 worth of stock ($50 x 100 shares = $5,000).

But if Bell Telephone declares a 2-for-1 stock split, then your 100 shares of stock will become 200 shares. But that means the par value will be reduced by half. If the par value is $1 per share, then after the split, it will be 50 cents per share. Also, the current selling price (market price) of the shares will be reduced by half (50 percent) to $25 (from $50).

On the surface, you have not done much better with the stock split than you have with the stock dividend: You have more shares, but each share is worth less. It is much like someone giving you two dollars but saying that from now on each one is worth only 50 cents.

Before the split:
You own 100 shares at $50 per share = $5,000

After the split:
You own 200 shares at $25 per share = $5,000

However, there can be benefits to the investor from a stock split. Before and after the split, you have $5,000 worth of stock. But after the split, you have more shares—twice as many, even if their total value is still only $5,000.

"But I have no more money than before!" you cry out. "I've been swindled!" It only seems that way until you realize the advantages of a stock split.

Before you had only 100 shares, so each time the shares went up $1, you would make only $100 ($1 x 100 shares). But now you have 200 shares, so each time the stock goes up $1, you will make $200 ($1 x 200 shares).

Of course, if the stock goes down, you will lose twice as much money with each decline in price. And usually a stock will decline in price shortly after a stock split. So why have a stock split? Because in the majority of cases, the price declines only for a short period, then it eventually climbs higher.

But there are no guarantees. *There are never any guarantees in the stock market.*

If there is a cash dividend associated with stock before it splits, the cash dividend will also be reduced:

Before 2-for-1 split:
Dividend = $1.00 per share

After 2-for-1 split:
Dividend = $0.50 per share

Sometimes a company will increase the dividend per share when a stock is split.

The main purposes of a stock split are to give shareholders a chance to profit more because they have additional shares and to increase investor interest in the stock through the new and lower price. It is anticipated by management that the lower price of the stock after the split will make it more affordable to the investment community. The more interest in the stock, the greater its price will rise. And as a stockholder, you always want the price of your stock to go up.

The company declaring the stock split benefits in two unique ways. It has a chance to give something to its stockholders without it costing the corporation any more than administrative expenses. And if the stock split results in increased value of the shares, when the company issues more stock, it can issue it at a higher price.

Stock splits may occur in any ratio. You will often hear of 3-for-2 or 3-for-1 splits or even other combinations.

Sometimes, corporations will declare a reverse split. This means that instead of getting, say, 2 shares for every 1 that you own, you get 1 share for every 2 that you own. Whereas you may have owned 100 shares before the 1-for-2 reverse split, you will have only 50 shares afterward.

Before the reverse split:
You own 100 shares at $50 per share = $5,000

After the split:
You own 50 shares at $100 per share = $5,000

In the case of the reverse split, everything happens in just the opposite way from for a regular split. You have half as many shares, but now the market value of each share is doubled (as well as the par value). Dividends, if they are being paid, will also double on each share. Reverse splits may be 1-for-2, 1-for-3, 2-for-3, or in any ratio that the corporation feels to be advantageous.

The reason for reverse splits is to increase the market value of each share because if a stock price is too low, people may be afraid to buy it for fear that the corporation issuing the stock is not doing well. So, the reverse split is a sort of psychological ploy.

You will find, however, that reverse splits are very rare. This is because corporations realize that a reverse split might rightly or wrongly be judged as a response to financial difficulties, and stock prices may suffer.

Stock Quotations

Table 4-1 gives a typical listing of stock quotations. You will find quotes like these in the business sections of daily newspapers or in the trading sections of financial publications. Internet financial sites will also list stock trades in similar format, although the Internet listings are usually much more detailed.

There is no one format. Some quote listings are highly abbreviated, some greatly expanded in terms of the data they provide. In all cases, however, stock listings are for common stocks unless otherwise indicated.

Stock Prices

Stock quotations are usually given in sixteenths, eighths, fourths, and halves of a dollar.

Table 4-1
Typical Stock Quotations

52-Week High	52-Week Low	Stock	Div	Yld %	PE Ratio	Sales 100s	High	Low	Last	Change
39 3/4	22 7/8	Alcan	.60	1.5	26	15922	40	41	41 1/16	+ 1/16
45	20 3/8	Alcatel	.43	1.0	14	5912	44	42	43 7/16	+ 1 9/16
14	5	AlidHldg	....	....	34	687	6 7/8	5 7/8	6 1/16	....
168 7/8	94 7/8	AmExp	.90	.5	32	9422	165	163	165	+2 1/4
25 3/4	19 7/8	AmExp pfA	1.97	8.7	....	573	21	20	20 1/8	....

Sometimes they are given in other fractions. *One day soon all listings will be in decimal.*

The fractional values and their monetary values are given below:

$\frac{1}{16}$	=	6 $\frac{1}{4}$ cents		$\frac{2}{16}$ ($\frac{1}{8}$)	=	12 $\frac{1}{2}$ cents
$\frac{3}{16}$	=	18 $\frac{3}{4}$ cents		$\frac{4}{16}$ ($\frac{1}{4}$)	=	25 cents
$\frac{5}{16}$	=	31 $\frac{1}{4}$ cents		$\frac{6}{16}$ ($\frac{3}{8}$)	=	37 $\frac{1}{2}$ cents
$\frac{7}{16}$	=	43 $\frac{3}{4}$ cents		$\frac{8}{16}$ ($\frac{1}{2}$)	=	50 cents
$\frac{9}{16}$	=	56 $\frac{1}{4}$ cents		$\frac{10}{16}$ ($\frac{5}{8}$)	=	62 $\frac{1}{2}$ cents
$\frac{11}{16}$	=	68 $\frac{3}{4}$ cents		$\frac{12}{16}$ ($\frac{3}{4}$)	=	75 cents
$\frac{13}{16}$	=	81 $\frac{1}{4}$ cents		$\frac{14}{16}$ ($\frac{7}{8}$)	=	87 $\frac{1}{2}$ cents
$\frac{15}{16}$	=	93 $\frac{3}{4}$ cents				

Column Headings

Using the last two stock listings in Table 4-1 as our references when necessary, let's look at what the columns represent.

52-Week High. This price of $25.75 is the highest price at which American Express Preferred A stock has sold in the last 52 weeks. If the stock closed at $26 for the day, the 52-week high would still show $25.75 until the next day's listing. There are a number of different types of preferred stock that a corporation might issue, as discussed earlier. Some are cumulative, some callable, some participating, some convertible, some a combination.

They are usually identified by alpha characters (letters of the alphabet).

52-Week Low. This price of $19.87 is the lowest price at which American Express Preferred A stock has sold in the last 52 weeks. If the stock closed at $18 for the day, the 52-week low would still show $19.87 until the next day's listing.

Stock. In this column, you will find the name of the stock or an abbreviation of its name.

Div. This amount indicates the total annual dividend the company has declared in the last 52 weeks. As you can see by the dividend of American Express common and preferred stocks in Table 4-1, preferred stocks usually pay higher rates of return.

P/E Ratio. This is the price-to-earnings ratio. It is determined by dividing the current price of each share of common stock by the earnings per share. Look at the next-to-last listing in Table 4-1, which shows the American Express common. The P/E ratio of 32 means that the price of the stock is selling at 32 times the earnings of each share.

The P/E ratio is a very general guide that tells investors whether or not a stock is overpriced. However, what is a good P/E ratio for a stock in one industry may not be a good one for a stock in another industry. So, unless you know the stock very well, and know a lot about its marketplace and trading history, the P/E ratio will have very little meaning for you.

However, if you are interested in knowing what the earnings per share actually are, you can find out by dividing the closing price of the stock ($165) by the P/E ratio of 32. Your answer would be $5.16 per share.

Sales 100s. The number you find in this column represents the number of shares that have been traded for the stock. Simply multiply the number given by 100. Thus, the number of shares traded for American Express common is 942,200 (9422 x 100); and for the preferred stock it is 57,300 (573 x 100).

High, Low, Last. The values in these columns represent the trading ranges of the stock for the period covered—usually a full trading day.

Change. The number in this column indicates the difference between this day's closing price and the previous trading day's. If no value is given, then there has been no change in the closing prices.

Information and Evaluation

Many new investors believe they can make a decision to buy or sell a stock simply on the information given in stock quotations, such as the example we have used in Table 4-1. But nothing could be further from the truth. Stock quotations simply give a snapshot of a particular stock's recent performance. A great deal of research should be carried out before you make a decision to buy or sell a particular stock.

The table we have just looked at really tells us little about American Express as a company. It simply tells us what its trading ranges have been for the year and for the day, how many shares were recently traded, and what the dividend and yield might be.

There is much more to know about the stock before it should be purchased or sold.

What are the company's future prospects? Will sales continue to grow? Will profits continue to grow? Will management remain strong and decisive? Will its national and international markets continue to expand? Are there major competitors ready to take away some of its business? Will it continue to pay a dividend?

These are just some of the questions that must be asked. The stock listings (or stock quotes) do not answer these questions. They are simply a scorecard.

All that stock listings can do is bring to your attention stocks that you may want to investigate for purchase or sale. They can do no more.

Be smart. Do not buy a stock because of what it did yesterday or over the previous year.

Buy a stock because of what it can do tomorrow and the next day. Buy it for what it will do in the future.

Making and
Losing
a Zillion

Investors enjoy making their money work for them. That means they want to use their money to earn even more money. Some people accomplish this by putting money in a bank where it will grow slowly but always safely.

Others prefer to try and make as much money as they can, so they invest it in the stock market—even though there is a chance they can lose all of it. These people include stock traders and stock investors. Unlike people who put their money in the bank, stock investors and traders are risk takers. And they know that the more money they want to try and make, the greater the risks they will have to take.

You were briefly introduced to stock trading in chapter 1. Now it is time to look more deeply into what it is all about. Let's first look at a very simple example of how money is made on an investment.

Buying Long

Suppose that you have a baseball autographed by a famous baseball player. And suppose that you paid $100 for the baseball.

Now I come along and I want that baseball—so badly that I am willing to pay you $200 for it. If you sell it to me, you will make $100.

You sold the baseball for: $200
You paid for the baseball: $100
Your profit: $100

It is just basic arithmetic. You made $100 because you were smart enough to sell the baseball for more than you paid for it. That's called buying low and selling high. If you paid $200 for the baseball and sold it for only $100, then you would lose $100. Simple subtraction tells you that.

Now let's look at how money is made on a stock investment. Suppose that instead of investing in that baseball, on February 1 you invested $10,000 in shares of stock in PepsiCo, Inc. That is the company that makes Pepsi Cola. Now suppose that by the following June, business has been so great for PepsiCo that people are willing to pay you $20,000 for your ownership shares in

the company. If you decide to sell your holdings, you will make $10,000.

> You sold your ownership in PepsiCo for: $20,000
> You bought ownership in PepsiCo for: $10,000
> Your profit: $10,000

Why would someone be willing to pay you more for PepsiCo stock than you paid for it? Because they believe business will continue to be good for PepsiCo, and they will be able to sell their stock for even more money at a future date—maybe even one minute after they buy it. Stocks do not always go up, however.

Or they may expect that PepsiCo will continue to increase dividends and they want the income from those dividends.

There you have it! The formula for making money in the stock market: Buy low, sell high.

When you buy a stock in the hope of selling it later at a higher price, you are said to have made a regular way trade. This is also called "buying long."

Selling Short

Now you do not have to buy first, then sell, in order to make money. In the stock market you can sell first, then buy. But the formula for success (making a profit) still remains the same: Buy low, sell high.

Selling first, then buying back the stock at a later date (or possibly just seconds or minutes later) is called short selling. Buying the stock back is called "covering your position." Investors who engage in short selling are called bears. A bear is expecting or hoping the particular stock (or the stock market in general) will go down. A bull, by contrast, expects a stock (or the market in general) to go up.

Does this mean that you can sell a stock you do not own? Yes, it most certainly does.

Short selling is done when you feel the price of a stock is going to go down and you want to make money when it does so. You see, in the stock market, you can make money when a stock goes up or goes down. Not everyone knows this.

For example, consider again PepsiCo stock. Suppose you feel the stock is going to go down $50 per share.

On July 1, you call your broker and tell him or her you want to sell short 100 shares of the stock at its current price—$100 per share. (100 shares x $100 per share = $10,000.) The broker borrows the shares from someone else's account—maybe his or her own—and lends them to you for you to sell. Basically, what you are doing is selling stock that you have borrowed by promising to pay for it later.

You called it right! By August 1, the stock drops by $50 per share and the shares you own are worth only $5,000 (100 shares x $50 = $5,000). So you cover your position by buying back the stock. Your broker now returns the shares to the other person's account.

When all the paper shuffling is done, you have made $5,000. Again, it is just simple arithmetic:

You bought 100 shares of PepsiCo for: $ 5,000
You sold 100 shares of PepsiCo for: $10,000
Your profit: $ 5,000

Even though this was a short sale and not a regular way trade, you still stuck to the formula for success: Buy low, sell high. The only difference is that you sold first, then bought.

But, like most things, buying low and selling high is easy to say and very, very hard to do. You have to be able to predict the way in which the stock is going to move—down for short selling, and up for regular way trades. If the stock goes in the opposite direction than you expect it to go, you will lose money.

Making and Losing Money

It is not easy to find a stock that is going to be profitable, whether you are a regular way trader or a short seller. That is why successful stock investors and stock traders always do a great deal of studying before they pick a stock in which to invest.

Look below at Table 5-1. It shows five trades made by a zillionaire.

Table 5-1
Keeping Track of Stock Transactions

Stock	Purchase Date	# of Shares	Cost*	Sell Date	Price*	Profit or (Loss)*
AT&T	1/20	1000	1	4/20	2	1
Lucent	1/21	2000	1½	4/22	2½	1
Bell Atlantic	2/04	5500	5	5/06	4½	(½)
Disney	2/06	8000	10	5/25	15	5
ExxonMobil	4/10	6000	14	7/11	12	(2)
			31½		36	4½

* Numbers represent "zillions" of dollars.

The price column minus the cost column should equal the profit and loss column. Values in parentheses indicate a negative value, or loss.

You may ask, of course, who has a zillion dollars?

No one, really.

A zillion is not really a number. It represents an unspecified amount. To a schoolboy or schoolgirl with no

money of his or her own, a hundred dollars could be like a zillion dollars. A zillion dollars is more money than you can count, more than you will ever have.

For you and me, it represents the money we wish we had to invest.

So, in Table 5-1, which illustrates some important lessons about stock trading, we deal in zillions of dollars. This is the money we wish we had to invest so we can make the kind of money we would like to spend.

What are the important lessons in Table 5-1?

1. Not all trades are successful.
2. You can buy any amount of shares that you can afford.
3. You can keep stock for as long as you want.
4. Profits and losses are determined by simple arithmetic.
5. This is the information you need to keep track of for tax purposes because you must pay taxes on the money you make trading stocks.

There is much to learn about the stock market. A lot of research goes into selecting the right stock and deciding whether you should play the stock to go up (buy long) or go down (sell short).

There is still much that you have to learn, but if you really study the examples in Table 5-1, you will see that the true secret of success in the stock market is:

Buy low. Sell high.

GLOSSARY

asking price The lowest price at which a stock is offered for sale.

bid price The highest price at which someone is willing to buy a stock.

common stock Generally, stock that gives its owner voting and profit-sharing rights.

dividends Share of a corporation's net earnings that is paid to stockholders. Sometimes, however, dividends are a share of past rather than current earnings.

preferred stock A security that has some of the characteristics of common stock and some of the characteristics of a bond. (A stockholder is an owner of a corporation; a bond holder is a creditor of the corporation.)

shares Term sometimes used to denote a unit of stock, sometimes used as a synonym for stock.

short sale A stock trade in which an investor profits by selling a stock or security and then buying it back (covering his or her position) at a future date. A strategy popular with "bears."

yield Return on investment. For instance, if you buy stock for $100 and receive $15 in dividends every year, your yield is 15 percent (.15 x $100).

FOR MORE INFORMATION

Buying virtual shares
http://library.thinkquest.org/10326/market_simulation/ifk.html
Play the stock market without spending any money.

Main Xchange
http://www.MainXchange.com/stockgame
A simulated stock market.

Money Management
http://www.YoungBiz.com
Provides information on money management, entrepreneurship, and investing
for teens.

Young Investors Network
Salomon Smith Barney
http://www.salomonsmithbarney.com/yin
Learn how to plan a budget and make decisions with your parents and investment professionals about investing in securities.

The Young Investor's Website
Liberty Financial Company
http://www.younginvestor.com/pick.shtml
Download or play on-line educational games such as the Money-Tration
memory game or the Young Investor trivia game.

FOR FURTHER READING

Dalton, John M. *How the Stock Market Works*. Englewood Cliffs, NJ: Prentice-Hall, 1993.

Draze, Diane. *Stock Market Game: A Simulation of Stock Market Trading*. San Louis Obispo, CA: Dandy Lion Publications, 1998.

Gilpatric, C. Edward. *Cliffs Notes Investing in the Stock Market*. Indianapolis, IN: IDG Books, 1999.

Godin, Seth. *If You're Clueless About the Stock Market and Want to Know More*. Chicago, IL: Dearborn Trade, 1997.

Holloway, Clark. *Stock Market 101*. Fremont, CA: Jain, 1996.

Kelly, Jason. *The Neatest Little Guide to Stock Market Investing*. New York: Plume, 1998.

INDEX

CREDITS

About the Author

Charles Caes is a stock investor and options trader, as well as the author of books on investment and science. He holds an MBA from Averett College, an Ed. M. from Columbia University, and a BS from Seton Hall University. His other published works on the market are for active securities traders and include *Tools of the Bull, Tools of the Bear, Stock Market Arithmetic: A Home Study Guide,* and *Covered Calls: The Safest Game in the Options Market.* He resides in Virginia with his wife Karen.

Photo Credits

Cover photos © Artville; p. 22 © Joe Outland/Uniphoto Picture Agency; p. 24 © Scott Thode/International Stock Photography; p. 33 © Inge Yspeert/Corbis; p. 37 © Kit Kittle/Corbis; p. 38 © Bill Losh/FPG; p. 42 © Superstock.

Series Design

Law Alsobrook

Layout

Cynthia Williamson